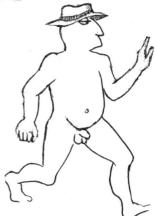

The Joy of Letting Women Down

The Joy of Letting Women Down

SECRETS OF THE WORSHIPPED MALE

Natalie d'Arbeloff

Robson Books

First published in Great Britain in 2000 by Robson Books, 10 Blenheim Court, Brewery Road, London N7 9NT

A member of the Chrysalis Group plc

British Library Cataloguing in Publication Data
A catalogue record for this title is available from the British Library

ISBN 1–86105–376–2

Typeset by FiSH Books, London
Printed and bound in Great Britain by Creative Print & Design (Wales), Ebbw Vale

CONTENTS

FOREWORD

**womaniser philanderer adulterer
libertine rake roué lecher
bed-hopper fornicator profligate
lady-killer**

According to rumour, the above are a dying species if not actually extinct. No self-respecting woman wants to be seen dead with one of these dinosaurs of a by-gone phallocentric age. Prominent members of the breed have been spotted lining up at the clinics of eminent therapists to be cured of what has now been identified as the serious disease of 'Sex Addiction'. Sufferers are begging to be reformed, re-framed, re-programmed to be reborn as New Men...

Really?

So why is the Womaniser never short of willing women? Why does the Adulterer make whoopee with adulteresses, the Philanderer with philanderines and the Rake with rakettes? Why are these women swarming around so-called dinosaurs? Are they all brainless bimbos? No doubt there are a few BB's among the female crowd leaving messages on the dinosaur's e-mail, fax and cell-phone. But there are also PhDs, MDs and VIPs of every description. How to explain this phenomenon? Evolution theory? So *that's* why women throw themselves at adulterous alcoholics, chain-smokers, gluttons, gamblers and absconding impregnators while nice guys with steady jobs, healthy bodies and caring-sharing ways frequently languish alone in the columns of personal ads?

Evolution schmevolution! Something else is going on here and you are about to find out what it is.

INTRODUCTION

- Most women want a man they can worship.(*)
- Most women want a man they can rely on. (*)
- It's a fact of life that those two things are incompatible:
- Men who are worshipped are not reliable.(*)
- And men who are reliable are not worshipped.(*)

Another fact you may have noticed is that women tend to *flock* towards the worshipable man (WM) whereas they merely *trickle* towards the reliable man (**rm**).

This book is about and for the man who is *flocked* to, the **WORSHIPPED MALE**. It is not suggesting that being a WM is a good thing. It is a very bad thing which, like many bad things, is also a lot of fun. This book reveals

---

(*) Sweeping statements will be made throughout this book.

precisely why this bad thing is fun and precisely why this fun is bad.

- If you are – or want to be – the kind of man who is worshipped, read on.
- If you are a reliable man, look away now before you become corrupted.
- If you are a woman in thrall to a WM, learn the tricks of his trade.
- If you are casualty of too-close encounters with WMs, this book will bring back memories.
- If you have never met a WM, don't worry: sooner or later you will.

Let this be an introduction.

1

HOW IT BEGAN

Before that apple business, Adam and Eve were buddies, gambolling around the Garden with the other animals like a couple of kids and if they had sex at all, it was innocent sex.

Then sly old Satan, dressed up as a snake, wriggled up to Eve, handed her the apple and aroused her curiosity with a seductive '*WOW*! You have *never* tasted *anything* like *this*!'

So she bit. And she tasted. And suddenly Eve looked at Adam and no longer saw her buddy: she saw a god – the very first **WORSHIPABLE MAN**. And she was well and truly hooked.

And Eve said to Adam: 'Have a taste of *THIS*!'

And Adam tasted. And he felt a warm, sexy power racing through his veins. And he looked into Eve's eyes and saw what *she* saw: himself as a god. And he fell in love with this reflection.

And old Satan was laughing up his snakeskin sleeve and licking his chops in anticipation of the scene that was to follow.

What was that?

You guessed it:

THE BIG BANG!

And the same scene, with variations, is replayed every time a woman looks at a WM and every time a WM looks at himself in a woman's eyes.

So now you know why **WORSHIPABLE MAN** is here to stay, even if a minority of the daughters of Eve and the sons of Adam are running around with placards insisting that everything should go back to *HOW IT WAS BEFORE THE APPLE.*

2

ADDICTABILITY

The key to worshipability is **SEX APPEAL** – not as in 'Isn't that baby's smile appealing?' but as in the command *'I APPEAL TO YOUR SEX!'* Call it charisma, animal magnetism, *je ne sais quoi* – WM's appeal goes straight to the genitals, by-passing the brain.

If you've got **IT** you know you've got it but even if you weren't born with it, you may still be able to acquire it by applying the methods in this book.

If you are a WM, you have been using these methods instinctively for years but now you can refine your technique and learn some new tricks, as well as how to recognise the dangers which could threaten your status.

If you happen to have brooding good looks, with a hint of menace in the curl of the lip, the tilt of the eyebrows, then that's a bonus. But handsomeness is by no means a prerequisite to worshipability.

History shows that WMs past and present, famous and infamous, have often been of the short, fat, skinny or bald variety – and what's more, they are not always rich: quite a few earn a lot less that the ladies who worship them. Neither is age an impediment – you need only look around! Many a WM has been seen to acquire greater worshipability the older and more outrageous he becomes in exercising his power, that power all WMs have in common and in abundance:

SEXUAL POWER

Does this mean that every WM is a great lover? Or exceptionally well-hung? Or that he can keep it up for an unusually long time? No, no and no! There are bound to be some WMs who do indeed possess one or more of these qualifications but they are the exception rather than the rule.

Research has proved that the majority of WMs are about average – and occasionally, below average – in the above department. So, what exactly is this power?

It is **ADDICTABILITY** – the ability to cause women to become sexually addicted to them.

This is a skill nurtured and honed by many years of practise, which is why young WMs rarely excel at it – unless they started very early indeed.

The basic law of **ADDICTABILITY** is summed up in this slogan:

> *FIRST A HIT*
> *THEN A MISS*
> *OVER AND OVER*
> *LEADS TO BLISS*

You create and prolong addiction in your worshippers by unexpectedly (unexpected is important) giving something pleasurable and following it up with an unexplained (unexplained is important) refusal or withdrawal. You then repeat the process for as long as you wish to keep a woman addicted.

To illustrate this technique in action, here is an actual case-history (names and places have been changed).

Marcia is one of the employees in the office of George, a well-known WM. Quietly and unobtrusively, she worships the ground he walks on but he has not done any more than give her the occasional conspiratorial smile when he passes her desk. One morning, on a whim, he decides to take her along on a quick business trip to Paris. He sends her instructions via e-mail to meet him at the airport. Marcia dashes home to pack a bag and arrives at the airport on time, breathless and ecstatic. George turns up only seconds before boarding. The flight is a blur of vodka-fuelled sexy banter and by the time their taxi pulls up at the Paris hotel, Marcia is sure they are going straight to bed and bliss. However, at reception, George books two non-adjoining rooms and says he'll meet her in the bar in an hour. Disappointed but still hopeful, Marcia re-washes her hair, re-applies her make-up, changes her clothes and goes down to the bar to wait for her Master. Two hours late, George arrives, all smiles, orders drinks to be sent to his room and taking Marcia's arm, invites her to come up and see his contracts. In his room, Marcia discovers this was no double-entendre: he gives her a stack of documents to proofread while he disappears into the bathroom. She tries to concentrate on the task, heart pounding, waiting, anticipating. George takes his time then asks her to bring him a drink. Lolling in the bubble bath, eyes closed, he commands her to sit down and take dictation. Marcia obeys, struggling to maintain secretarial composure, but suddenly it's all too much – the alcohol, the steam, and especially the naked nearness of her god – the business words spilling from his sacred lips make no sense to her at all. She leans over him, whispering hoarsely: 'Take me!' or words to that effect.

George's response is icy: she has interrupted his important train of thought; and what makes her presume to be on intimate terms with him? He is regretting having brought her along. Marcia dissolves in tears, begs forgiveness. George tells her to go back and finish the proofreading while he resumes his bathtub cogitations alone. Marcia, now on automatic pilot, does as she is told.

Eventually, George emerges and announces that she now deserves a break: dinner at his favourite Brasserie.

In the taxi, he puts his arm around her, teases her, calls her Jezebel. At the restaurant he is warmly greeted, particularly by a very pretty, very nubile waitress who evidently knows him well. All through the meal, while Marcia tries valiantly to make conversation, George's attention wanders in the direction of the waitress. Defeated, Marcia announces she has a migraine and is going back to the hotel to sleep. George orders a taxi for her, says he wants to stay and have coffee; he'll see her in the morning.

Back in her room, Marcia cries herself to sleep. Some time in the small hours, there's a knock on her door: it is George, much the worse for booze and bonk, pretending he has lost the key to his room. Marcia lets him in and he climbs into bed beside her. Though sated, George always has room for a little dessert: he places Marcia's head over his Worship and, denied for so long, she does a very efficient worshipping job indeed. Offering no extras whatsoever, after a short restorative sleep, George is out of her room and back in his own before she can get sentimental.

The next day on the flight back home, George is in jocular mood but there is no mention of the incident and no hint of intimacy. As soon as the plane lands, he rushes off. His parting words 'Don't be late at the office!'

Marcia goes back to work, shattered, but also high on adrenaline, elation, frustration, love and rage. She has been transformed from a mere worshipper to a complete addict in approximately 48 hours.

This true story serves as a Master Class in **ADDICTABILITY**. To appreciate the expertise and speed with which George uses the HIT/MISS rule, let us list the essential points in the scenario:

1. Unexpected invitation to Paris – **HIT**
2. Let her wait at airport – **MISS**
3. Intimate chat during flight – **HIT**
4. Separate rooms; keep her waiting – **MISS**
5. Invite her to his room and to his bath-time – **HIT**

6. Reject her advances – **MISS**
7. Tease her, take her to dinner – **HIT**
8. Flirt with waitress, remain at restaurant, screw waitress – **MISS**
9. Surprise visit to M's bed afterwards; let her have a taste – **HIT**
10. But keep it strictly business, no extras – **MISS**

As you see, it is the tantalising see-saw manipulation of the worshipper's desire which builds dependence, guaranteeing WM's power over her. If this seems astonishing, you may still be at the adolescent stage of worshipability (whatever your age), when impatience rules. You would do well to memorise the following precepts:

a) Never satisfy when you can keep in suspense.
b) Never let a woman feel secure with you.
c) Never underestimate the aphrodisiac power of disappointment.
d) When you have her on a string, picking her up and letting her down are as easy as Yo-Yo.

WHEN YOU HAVE HER
ON A STRING

PICKING HER UP
AND LETTING HER
DOWN

ARE AS EASY
AS YO-YO

3

THE MANAGEMENT OF FEMALE LUST AND JEALOUSY

Do you still cling to that old myth about the male of the species being randier than the female? If so, wake up to the truth: Women are not only randier than men but female lust, when directed at a WM, is far more intense and longer-lasting than the male's.

Even the most promiscuous, energetic WM's libido has limits – it can be instantly turned on by any number of desirable objects but once he has satisfied his lust, it's turned off until the next stimulus comes along. Not so for a fully addicted female: she is able to remain in a state of intense erotic arousal almost indefinitely, with or without the presence of her WM, with or without sexual satisfaction.

However, her lust is not transferable: if *YOU* are her WM, then *YOU* and only *YOU* are her lust-object. She may have a spouse or other lovers but her erotic chemistry, once hooked, concentrates on you exclusively. This can be a source of great pleasure for you, but also of danger.

For a demonstration of the frightening force of female lust on a mass scale, you have only to look at the screaming, sobbing, throbbing, grabbing, writhing girls and women in the audience of any worshipped male entertainer or leader, past or present. And although their erotic hysteria may be collective, every one of these females feels she is alone with her god and is begging him to have his way with her, *OR ELSE*! Some really expert guru-type WMs can maintain an entire community of women in a state of permanent arousal and, thus entranced, they will accept the most intolerable conditions, the most irrational demands, just to remain within the aura of their WM.

Your status as a WM means that you are, at all times, at the centre of a circle – large or small, depending on your influence – of addicted and addictable women. And women are prone to jealousy. And therefore you must learn to protect yourself from the inevitable effects of the jealousy and lust which you unleash.

Female jealousy ranks along with law suits and impotence as a major threat to your position. What with good lawyers and Viagra, the first two can be managed. But an army of jealous women is a bit harder to handle. They are cunning, implacable, unpredictable, and have espionage techniques MI6, FBI, CIA and KGB haven't even heard of. You have to think ahead, anticipate the moves a woman might make against you, given half a chance.

Does this mean that WM is calculating and suspicious?

Well yes, as a matter of fact, it does.

You have to be, in order to survive.

You didn't get to be what you are by good behaviour and although you may seem to be carefree, you must always be watchful in case any of your misdeeds catch up with you.

No hide-out is absolutely safe, no pleasure wholly untainted by fear of retribution. Even in your wildest moments of abandon, a sudden noise, a telephone ringing, a doorbell, might mean the game is up. Your partner in crime at the time may not understand why you are ever on guard – she may even be the type who chirps: '*so what* if we're found out? I *want* the whole world to know!'

No words have ever had a more powerful anti-aphrodisiac effect. You are out that door, forevermore.

Life as WM isn't all fun and games – it's a tough, nerve-wracking, knife-edge existence, and that's what you love about it. You are a rule-breaker but you have to learn the rules of *YOUR* game, the WM game, to perfection.

The cardinal rule of JEALOUSY MANAGEMENT is:

SPECIAL RELATIONSHIPS
or: **NEVER DUPLICATE**

Think of all the women in your circle as a team and visualize the different tasks or services that

each of them performs for you – or might perform for you, if you are considering new applicants. Give some thought (even if it's an effort) to the individual characteristics of each member, her particular contribution to your life, your pleasures, your work. Keep a private list (perhaps written in code) of the different assets which each of your women represents in your portfolio, as it were, of investments. This can serve as an aide-memoire when you are with a particular woman, helping you to establish the **Special Relationship** which is your insurance against the potential disasters of un-managed jealousy.

The **Special Relationship** principle works like this:

Every woman in your circle (except the very naive or very stupid) knows that there are other women in your circle. She may or may not have met the others personally but she is aware that they exist and she doesn't like that fact one little bit. It is a threat to her position, her sense of being uniquely chosen by you. And the more threatened she feels, the less unique, the more dangerous she becomes.

So: you convince her that she *is* unique; she is the *only one* who … (refer to your list and insert whatever it is she has/does that the others don't have/do). You cannot simply invent this on the spur of the moment – she will be able to spot a shallow compliment a mile away. You have to perform quite a tricky feat of diplomacy which, while giving nothing away about the other women, persuades this one that you and she have something *special* together, something you have never had with anyone else.

Okay, it's not easy to find what exactly is different, especially when it may not be all *that* different. But you've got to try: your security might depend on it.

If you can maintain that **Special Relationship** situation with every woman in your circle and never make her role interchangeable or similar, you've got a good chance of escaping the slings and arrows of outrageous jealousy.

But you may have to make some sacrifices: if, after careful examination, you discover that there are indeed some duplicates in your entourage, sorry, but you'll have to let the carbon-copies go.

Variety is the spice of life, yes! But duplication is just gluttony. As well as inefficient management.

The following horror story from our files illustrates just what can happen when the **Special Relationship** principles are ignored:

Married WM Hugo shares partnership of an architectural firm with Samantha, who is also his regular mistress. Their personal and professional relationship has been functioning successfully for some time.

When a new employee, Denise, is hired to take on PR duties, no warning bells ring in Samantha's head. She has long since accepted Hugo's WM ways, secure in her special relationship with him. Besides, Denise is not particularly attractive and Hugo barely notices her. What Samantha does not know is that, for Denise, it was addiction at first sight upon meeting Hugo. Moreover, she is a very clever and determined woman and gradually, 'innocently', she insinuates herself into both Sam and Hugo's confidence, making herself indispensable at work. Slowly, there are more and more tête-a-tête conferences between Denise and Hugo when Samantha is not in the office. Too

astute to try overtly sexual tactics, Denise seduces Hugo by appealing to his ambition and vanity. She persuades him that his talent is unique and needs a unique opportunity, which she just happens to have lined up for him: a friend of hers, Toby, is a wealthy West Indian who wants to build a hotel on land he owns in the Caribbean.

Denise has spoken to him so highly of Hugo's genius that Toby has invited them (Denise and Hugo) to view the site, all expenses paid. There's just one thing, says Denise: as this is a personal invitation it would be awkward to bring Samantha along, so why not wait and tell her about this project *after* visiting the site? Hugo is aware of the flaws in this reasoning but, excited by the prospect of combining potentially lucrative business with pleasure (he has gradually become attracted to Denise, especially to her respectful admiration of his talent), he concocts a strategy: the trip is only for a weekend so he will tell Samantha that he is, as usual, spending it at home with his wife, Helen. And he will tell Helen that he has to attend a conference in Jamaica, simply omitting the fact that Denise is accompanying him. Helen is a sensible soul who has learned to keep her doubts under wraps, preferring not to rock the boat. She, too, feels secure in her special relationship with Hugo.

The illicit trip is arranged and the two accomplices gaily fly off to the Caribbean, oblivious to the chain of events their action is unleashing. As fate will have it, Samantha phones Hugo at home on that very weekend, needing to clarify a technical question.

Helen, who is friendly with Sam and unaware of the fact that she is more than a business partner to her husband, tells her that Hugo's gone to Jamaica; she is surprised that Sam doesn't know about the 'conference'. Pretending she simply forgot about it, Sam rings off and immediately begins her investigation. Back at the office, she finds incriminating evidence of the double betrayal: not only is Hugo two-timing her sexually with the 'loyal' Denise, he is also sharing with this bitch the private, sacred territory of creativity which heretofore belonged only to Samantha. When the full enormity of this discovery hits her, Sam's outrage is incandescent

and urgent. Armed with two-dozen cans of spray paint, she storms into Hugo's elegant loft-apartment (she has a key, as it is where she and her lover meet extra-curricularly) and proceeds to decorate every pristine minimalist square inch of it with obscene and indelible graffiti.

Next, she picks up the phone and calls Helen: she confesses bluntly that she has been her husband's mistress for the past seven years and what's more he's been deceiving her with lots of other women, the latest one being that bitch Denise who is with him *RIGHT NOW* in Jamaica and here's the telephone number of their hotel. Moving on swiftly to her next manoeuvre, Sam manages to track down millionaire Toby's phone number.

He has returned early to his home in London, leaving Hugo and Denise to finish their working weekend alone in Jamaica. Samantha introduces herself, astounded that Toby is unaware of her position as Hugo's business partner. She demands that they meet immediately to discuss the matter.

Anxious to clarify things since he is about to commission Hugo to design his hotel, Toby invites Samantha for a drink at his house. Putting on her most seductive and persuasive behaviour, she charms him into perceiving Hugo as an envious, devious and mediocre architect who refuses to give credit to her own greater, more original talent and who – in cahoots with the besotted Denise – is plotting to con Toby into giving him the job, though he is incapable of designing anything to such high standards...

Enough said! Samantha's revenge is sweet and lethal and things turn out very badly for everybody except her and Toby. The moral is:

NEVER, EVER IGNORE THE SPECIAL RELATIONSHIP RULES!

Where **FEMALE LUST** is concerned, the management problems are quite different. This stems from the fact that, whereas jealousy is never a pleasant experience, lust frequently is.

So when you become endangered by lust, it's not your lust you have to worry about, but the female in heat over you.

Remember: A **WM-addicted female can**

remain in a state of erotic arousal almost indefinitely. *THINK ABOUT IT*! This might be very nice when you want it but what about when you've had enough of it with *her* and want to move on but you just can't turn her *off*?

That's when the trouble starts.

Every WM worth his title has experienced some variation or other on the Fatal Attraction scenario:

You approach, or are approached by, a **Sextette** (sex-mad blonde, redhead, or brunette). She is sexy, bold, beautiful and unmistakably available. So available that she seems to pop up wherever you are with offers you can't possibly refuse. So you accept, excited by her insatiable pursuit of you, and you have one of those ring-a-ding fling things. But when it gets to the 'Goodbye dear and Amen', she's not having it: she categorically refuses to co-operate. You try cool, you try funny, you try kind, you try brutal, you try threatening – she still refuses to call it quits. So you try legal: you tell her that if she doesn't leave you alone you are going to sue her for sexual harassment. She laughs her head off – she knows what to do: she'll

sue *YOU* for sexual harassment. And she'll win! After all, you're a well-known womaniser, philanderer, adulterer, etc. while she's just a feisty, free, assertive, sexually liberated woman, isn't she?

If things have got that far, they've gone too far. You have only four choices:

1. **The Fatal Attraction Solution** (but decide if you can afford to spend a lot of time in prison).

2. **The Aversion Therapy Solution:** give her so much of what she wants that she'll get nauseated by you and back off (maybe).

3. **The Leave-The-Country Solution:** change your name, your appearance.

4. **The Marry-Her Solution:** see 'MARRIAGE WM-STYLE'.

4

THE WM BRAIN

The **Worshipped Man**'s brain has been analysed by experts who were astonished to find that it contains huge amounts of a chemical known as **ID** (**Invitamus Distractionibus**). This chemical, which in the normal or average brain takes up a maximum 25% of space, rises to 75% and even to a record 99% in exceptional WMs.

This explains WM's almost total immunity to the 'virtues' that normal brains are heir to, for example: commitment; continuity; consistency; conscience; etc. The excess **ID** flooding his brain-cells makes WM so hyper-susceptible to any form of distraction – animal, vegetable or mineral – that there simply isn't time or space for any of the above slow-growing traits to take root.

Now you understand why your explanations are not always as far-fetched as they might sound: you really *did* just pop round the corner to buy cigarettes and ended up in Hawaii. The **ID** in your brain forced you to be distracted by the almond-eyed young lady with a suitcase desperately trying to flag down a taxi right near where your car was parked and then made you offer to drive her to the airport where one distraction led to another until suddenly, you woke up in Honolulu.

The fact that you had absolutely no intention of walking out on your wife and dinner-guests that evening is neither here nor there. Distractions exist to be distracted by, so says the **ID** in your brain, and you can't contradict a chemical, can you?

As with most chemicals, however, there is a price to pay in side-effects. A major side-effect of high **ID** is Severe Megalomania: WM's heightened responsiveness to the infinite number of distractions that life offers gives him a sense of omnipotence and reckless curiosity. There's no scent he can't follow, no door he can't break down, no stone he can leave unturned. Therefore, even if he achieves real (as opposed to delusions of) grandeur momentarily, the next moment it self-destructs because his attention is incapable of *not straying*. Spectacular financial gains followed by spectacular bankruptcies, meteoric career rises followed by humiliating dismissals, scandals of every description erupting volcanically wherever he sets foot – this is *your* life, WM!

However, short of having your brain drained, there's not much you can do about it. So you learn to live with it – you develop exquisite expertise in the art commonly known as:

GETTING AWAY WITH IT

Most people have some degree of talent in this field but only WM brings it to Olympic heights of perfection.

'How does he get away with it?' These words are constantly being said about you, sometimes in enraged tones, but more often in awe or barely concealed envy.

The notorious gangster and the WM are – not

always but more often than you think – one and the same person.

Admit it: the only things that don't appeal to you about a life of *real* – as opposed to *virtual* – crime, are:

getting caught

getting killed

So you may have opted to limit your crime-career to swashbuckling shenanigans in bed and boardroom, but watch out.

There is a new type of police force, far more effective than the standard one, made up almost exclusively of angry women and envious **rms**. And they are watching *you*, night and day. They are responsible for all that misinformation, those rumours about dinosaurs, 'Sex Addiction', etc. They have no pity or sympathy for your excess **ID** predicament. If they catch you, they will sentence you to join **Men's Groups** where, for a hefty fee, you will be forced to run naked through the woods with other guys, endure 'bonding' rituals and risk heart attack by stewing in a 'Sweatlodge' packed like sardines with the other convicts. And that's not all: as you sweat and squirm, you will

be ordered to do something called 'Sharing Your Feelings'.

Do not, under any circumstances, allow yourself to be caught!

In the good old days, before these Amateur Police Persons (APP) crawled out of the woodwork waving their principles, you could freely exercise your rights, those rights that your WM ancestors fought for and won. The right to booze and batter, for instance.

Since time immemorial, boozing and battering have gone together like love and marriage – *especially* in love and marriage! You could get drunk, knock the little woman around a bit, and if you were a WM, nobody said a word, least of all the little woman. If you were not a WM but only an ordinary guy, you *might* get arrested if found out. But then you'd just be thrown into a normal prison by a normal policeman for a normal length of time.

But that's all changed and it's likely to change even more. If the APP have their way, there will be a **Men's Group Prison Camp** on the outskirts of every city, every town, every village.

And surveillance cameras will be installed in your home, your workplace, your secret rendez-vous places. If you are a man, you will be watched. And if you are a WM you will be hounded!

So, be warned: the battering will have to go. Strike it off your CV now. You might go a bit easier on the booze but that's optional. Don't let them 'talk you through' your battering bent: it doesn't matter whether you did it because you were drunk, or because she deserved it, or because she didn't, or because you were a battered child, or because you're a sadistic bastard. Just stop. You can always try to understand it later, if you must.

They might be able to invade your privacy but they can't take away your high **ID**. And as long as you've got your high **ID**, you'll find some new distraction. And because you're a WM, you'll get away with it.

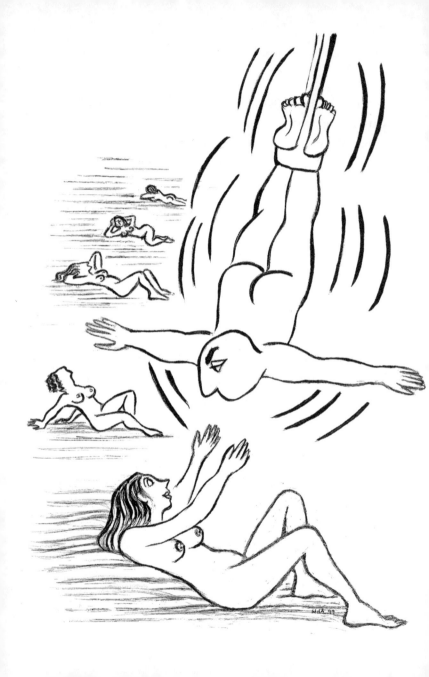

5

THE FALLING

Among the many unfair and inaccurate statements made about WM is that you are incapable of loving anyone because you love only yourself.

This fallacy is just that: the phallic envy of rejected women and un-flocked-to rms.

The truth is that you're incapable of *not* loving. What they cannot stomach is that you love serially, variably, and incontinently. And magnanimously: unlike ordinary people, you do not save yourself for parsimonious distribution to only a chosen few on the face of the earth. When so many freely offer you their devotion, why should you refuse them access, the opportunity to enter your orbit?

In the course of a typical day, your eyes will meet any number of potential love-objects who covertly or overtly signal their more-than-passing interest. What are you to do? Shut your eyes, your mind and all your senses simply because, at home or around the corner, a previously chosen one is waiting for you? Well, even if you wanted to, you can't, because of your high **ID**.

So, what you do is to fall. Others may Fall in Love but your expertise, your forte, is simply... **Falling**.

It is the parachute-jump, the risky, reckless, free-floating leap into the unknown that thrills you and endlessly tempts you. And when you're in full **Fall**, it must be said that nobody does it better. For every woman you perform your aerobatics for, it's the Coup de Foudre, the Real Turtle Soup. She feels that she is the only one you have ever fallen for in that particular way. She flies with you, she falls for you, she performs her own tricks for you, she knows she belongs to you, body and soul. What she doesn't know is that your love-fall is really a Bungee Jump: it doesn't end with a landing on terra firma – or in her arms forever – but in a bounce, right back up again then down again, in a new **Fall**… for somebody else.

However, while you are in **Falling** mode – whether it lasts an hour, a day, a month or a year (well, a year would be stretching it a bit) – you tend to believe you have found the *Perfect Woman*. Your Holy Grail always is the *Perfect Woman* but what you would do if you found her is not so clear.

What does the climber do when he's climbed Everest? He certainly doesn't want to spend the rest of his life up there turning into a block of ice! What he does is to look for another mountain, another challenge. In any case, it doesn't take long for your acute powers of observation to detect the flaws in one who had at first seemed to be the *Perfect Woman*. Perhaps she was deliberately concealing her imperfections; or perhaps they just became evident with familiarity. Whatever the reason, as soon as imperfection rears its ugly head, that's your cue to bounce up up and away. And the search is on again.

Romance, as practised by WM, bears no resemblance to anything imagined by Mills &

Boon. You receive Valentines, you never send them. Women offer you gifts of an intimate, sentimental or lavish kind; you ask them to give you some object of theirs which catches your fancy and which they really don't want to part with but will, since it's you. If you give gifts at all, they will be things you too can partake of and probably finish on the spot, such as a chicken, bottles of booze, etc. Your presence is the prime gift you bring to a woman and you see no reason for adding icing to that delectable cake.

You know that romance is what goes on (and on) in the head while sex is what goes on, for a limited time, in the bed – or anywhere else you happen to be. Women in general, as well as most rms and sentimentally or commercially driven film-producers, novelists and song-writers are obsessed with the idea that sex and romance *must* be combined, especially before and after orgasm. But WM knows that this combination is merely an option and it's one that he can choose to refuse. Who needs the nebulous, ephemeral, social-security benefits of romance when you have all the sex you want, on demand?

If a woman insists upon your uttering sentimental words or making sentimental gestures before, during, or after sex, tell her where to go: give her the telephone numbers of a few of your **rm** acquaintances, assuring her that they will be glad to fulfill her requirements. You might add that she can come back to you if ever she feels the need for Straight Sex – i.e. free from artificial additives, sweeteners, etc.

You can be sure that sooner or later she'll come running back even if in the meantime she's been wallowing in the arms of some knight in chocolate armour. The chocolate invariably melts, and then what does she see? Only some needy, dependent guy who *LURVES* her! She's no fool, she realises this is quite a useful accessory, especially if she's in the army of singles searching for security. But at this point, she'll want to have her cake and eat it, with you.

So she'll call you.

When she does, keep her waiting.

In any case, love is a problem.

You already have problems.

Do you really need another one?

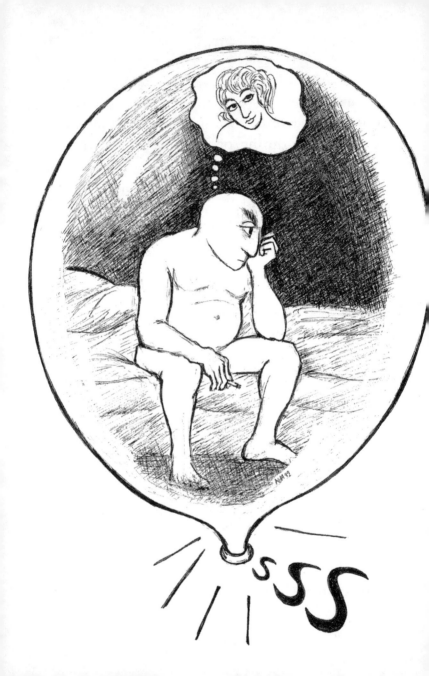

6

THE SSS

Try this experiment: Take a deep breath and, as you exhale, say 'SSS...' on a descending note.

With this sound of a balloon deflating, you have just demonstrated exactly what happens when the **SSS** hits you.

It might be on a cold, dark winter morning; or on a grey autumn afternoon; or even, unexpectedly, on a balmy summer evening. Suddenly, you experience a malaise, a deflated feeling. There may be an unspecific ache in the heart-region, queasiness in the stomach, cold in the hands and feet, and a vague longing for something, followed by sighing. As you sigh, the sense of longing increases and forms into a mental picture: a woman, a particular woman, perhaps one you had, and discarded, in the distant past – or perhaps one who is still within reach. The image becomes fused with the longing: *she* is the one who would have provided what your life lacks: for example, sincerity, stability, seriousness... **SSS** again!

STOP! Banish this image from your mind. It is only a hallucination. You are merely suffering from a bout of **Seasonal Sentimental Syndrome** and, like a cold, it will soon pass.

Above all, *DO NOT ACT* upon the feelings that are temporarily controlling you. Any moves you make, any decisions you take while afflicted by SSS will be bitterly regretted by you once you are back to your normal state of health. So *DO NOT* put on a sentimental record; *DO NOT* get drunk by yourself; *DO NOT* write a letter or make a long-distance phone call, and *DO NOT* under any circumstances buy an airline ticket or two to romantic places.

The best medicine for **SSS** is fast, instant and anonymous sex. Go out and find a willing stranger. If one isn't immediately available for free, hire one.

7

MARRIAGE WM-STYLE

Some useful definitions:

MIXED MARRIAGE
When you try to mix marriage with pleasure.
This is not a good mix as the two interfere with each other. Pleasure belongs outside of marriage and marriage is best kept in the home.

ARRANGED MARRIAGE
When you arrange for your wife to marry somebody else.

MARRIAGE OF CONVENIENCE
All your marriages are for your convenience.

MARRIAGE OF TRUE MINDS
When your wife tells you you have a better mind than hers and you agree that this is true.

OPEN MARRIAGE
She does what she likes, you do what you like and then you tell each other about it: *this does not work.* The only kind of marriage that can work for you is when you do what you like and don't tell her about it and she does what you like and shuts up about it.

MARRIAGE BUREAU
The locked bureau in your study where you keep things your wife mustn't see.

MARRIAGE COUNSELLOR
Somebody your wife needs to see.

The majority of WMs are divorced, about to divorce, or about to remarry. A good question is: Why does a WM marry at all? Here are some of the reasons:

- **Youthful Inexperience** – Some WMs are late-developers and not fully aware of who they are until their middle years, when life-circumstances give them the confidence to express their true natures. When this happens, the little wife acquired in their callow youth becomes an embarrassment and is generally dumped, or traded in for a new model.

- **Career Move** – WM realises the benefits of having a trophy-wife and/or a secretary/PA/hostess-wife.

- **Fear of Old Age** – When the creaks and cracks and creases can no longer be ignored, some WMs decide they need the insurance of a competent nurse-wife. This may require the dismissal of a trophy-wife, who isn't up to the job.

- **Trapped** – When some determined female (e.g. Sextette) manages to trick WM into marrying her, using any number of devious manipulations and inducements.

- **Delusion** – When the *'Perfect Woman'* illusion persists long enough to persuade WM that he must marry her or she'll disappear.

If you have decided, for whatever reason, that a wife really is what you need, make sure that the candidate you have chosen doesn't know what the job actually entails. Before the wedding, it's best if she remains starry-eyed and ignorant of the fact that being a WM's wife is the worst possible position a woman in love can occupy. Reality and WM are never on the best of terms and, as soon as the particularly hard-edged reality of continuous cohabitation hits you, shattering the impressionistic picture of it which your imagination had painted, you begin – ever-so surreptitiously – to back out of it.

However, constant proximity to her Beloved endows the new wife with amazing extra-sensory powers and it's not long before she susses out that you are secretly trying to tunnel out of the love-nest she is working so hard to decorate with tender loving care. Depending on her personality, IQ, DNA, social class, star-sign, etc. she then chooses one or more of the following options:

1. THE MARTYR

She bides her time, doesn't ask questions, eats lots of chocolate, puts on or loses a lot of weight, suffers silently from mysterious ailments, forgives you time and time again, believes she is your anchor, your Woman, and that her patience will eventually change you. It doesn't. She sinks, you swim.

2. OTHER INTERESTS

She develops other interests: a career, a child, a garden, an animal, a cause, an intellectual, spiritual, artistic or social pursuit. Oddly enough, she rarely takes up the option of tit-for-tat revenge-lovers; while her libido is still firmly hooked on you, other offers are simply not tempting. If she does stray, it is out of desperation and most likely for keeps, to the arms of an **rm**.

3. THE THERAPIST

She appoints herself as your Therapist / Analyst / -Healer / Guru. Quietly, confidently, and at length, she explains to you why you behave as you do, where your Karma has been, what colour your aura is, what your mother did to you, what foods you should avoid. She reads inspirational books to you, gives you massages and Tantric lessons in sexuality. All of which you gratefully accept while thinking of other things. When you are out of the house and up to goddess-knows-what, she holds her crystals and tries to get in touch with your feelings. Then she goes through your pockets and your post, looking for evidence.

4. THE INTERROGATOR

She protests, she complains, she confronts, she interrogates, she *nags*...sometimes even *in public*! But she doesn't leave. *you* leave. She pursues. Or sues.

5. THE MANAGER

She becomes your Manager and takes over the

running, promotion and protection of your career. Not for her the cosy domesticities: you eat out together or order take-aways. She's good in bed and on the Board of Directors. She fights for your interests tooth and perfectly manicured nail, makes and breaks appointments for you and plans your diary ten years ahead. If you die while this wife is in full swing, you are guaranteed excellent PR service to your memory for the rest of eternity.

Any woman you choose as wife or cohabitee must understand and abide by this basic rule: *Life with WM is about WM.*

It is not about her or about *Us* or *We*. To you, *we* is always the Royal We. 'What are we doing today?' means: 'What are you going to do for me today?'

If a woman can't cope with this rule, you'll know she's not your type.

Whatever their type, all WMs' wives or long-term cohabitees have one thing in common: ***SOONER OR LATER, THE WORSHIPFULNESS WEARS OFF.***

They can try to hide it from everyone – even from themselves – but the wearing off, like age, happens inexorably. This doesn't mean that their love and/or lust necessarily wears off, not at all. But the worship definitely goes. Suddenly, or very gradually, their very own god, their WM, looks like...well, just like an ordinary guy.

This is a very big problem. A tragedy. You may seem to be an insensitive brute in certain ways but you are gifted with a supernatural hyper-sensitivity to the tiniest fluctuations in the barometer of worship in your women. You *know*, you *see*, you *sense*, you *hear* – the blink of her eye, the catch in her voice, the flick of her hair, the twist of her hip: they're all signals, they're all the information you need to condemn her to a fate far worse than death (some are known to have preferred death by their own hand): *your indifference*.

When you have detected the unmistakable signs of her treason, that's IT, as far as you're concerned. You do not necessarily leave her – there may be practical advantages to keeping her around, or you may be too lazy for drastic

measures – but she ceases to exist within your private universe. She merely occupies a given space in your outer surroundings, like the bed, the television, or the exercise bike.

Though she has lost her worshipfulness, your unrelenting *indifference* is one thing a wife simply cannot cope with. So, in order to avoid this dreaded condition, she adopts a strategy: She lies. Not exactly lies, but becomes an expert at concealing the truth. Because she knows that your X-ray eyes can see through her, she performs a tour-de-force of acting ability: She acts the role of *herself as she was*, before her loss of worshipfulness.

Once in a blue moon, you are fooled. But, in general, this strategy has about as much chance of success as an atheist has of conning God into thinking he is a believer.

8

SLEEPING TOGETHER

This euphemism for sexual intercourse becomes, in marriage or cohabitation, a literal routine which you, as a WM, do not necessarily have to adopt.

Sleep is a private activity. Your snoring, your tosses and turns, your farting, your scratching, your dreaming, your duvet, are all yours. There is no law, written or unwritten, stating that you are obliged to share all these with another person who happens to be your spouse or live-in partner.

Opinion polls indicate that most people actually sleep better when sleeping alone; however, they also admit that is more convenient to have a partner in the same bed if horny feelings arise in the middle of the night or early morning.

Other surveys have revealed that both male and female sexual fantasies rarely feature a bed; and when asked to describe the most exciting sexual experiences of their lives, sleeping together was not mentioned at all by 95% of respondents.

Your sex-requirements and your sleep requirements are two entirely different matters. Do not be bamboozled by tradition or sentimentality or economy into lumping the two together willy-nilly. The wife or partner can sleep in the spare room. Or on the sofa.

9

TIME-MANAGEMENT AND EXCUSES

The only difference between the married and the freelance WM is the amount of time each has available for extra-curricular activity. As a free-lance, your 'curricular' activity may be simply work, your career. But as a married WM, it is your work *PLUS* your married life. Therefore, to enable you to fit in those indispensable extras, the efficient management of your time is not just an option but an imperative necessity.

If your marriage is shaky or already crumbling, you can afford to be a bit careless in your juggling. But if you have good reason to maintain the marital status quo, then there's no two ways about it, you've got to be

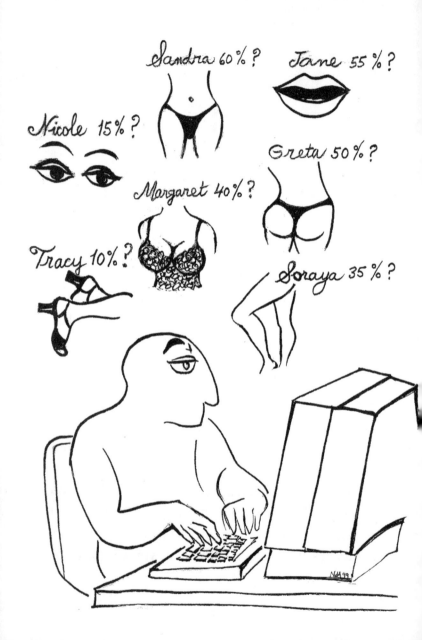

absolutely mathematical in working out your priorities.

A tried and tested method is as follows:

Divide your women into three categories -

A. **The Primary**
B. **The Regulars**
C. **The Temps**

Decide how much time you can afford to spend on each category. This is not unlike making a budget: you allot X-amount of money to spend per month or year – likewise, you have X-amount of time to spend as your desires, needs, health and circumstances allow. Of course there is never a guarantee that either money or time will be yours for long but, while you have them, you can choose how you want to use them.

The **Primary** generally requires the most predictable time-investment. In the average marital calendar, most nights, weekends and holidays are spent 'at home'. This means fitting in **Regulars** and **Temps** during working hours. If you are unemployed or unconventionally employed, you may have a more flexible time scale.

In any case, it is asking for marital bankruptcy if you find, when examining your WM-EXTRAS accounts at the end of the year, that 75% of your time was spent on **Temps**, 15% on **Regulars** and only 10% on your **Primary**. A more trouble-free time budget might look something like this:

Primary – 60%
Regulars – 30%
Temps – 10%

Of course unforeseen circumstances can completely wreck any budget. For example, a brief encounter with an exceptional **Temp** could turn into an extended encounter and reduce the time allotted to **Regulars** and even add to your stable of **Regulars** if you decide to upgrade the **Temp**. This in turn could upset the balance of the whole structure and have unwanted consequences.

The **Regulars**, if kept addicted and in line, tend to accept the unpredictable time changes that are your trademark. A long-term **Regular** might slam a door or hang up the phone on you but basically, she knows her place and won't do anything drastic. She doesn't have

the clout of a **Primary**, or the now-or-never lust-appeal of a **Temp**, so she concentrates on what keeps you returning to her, however erratically: her focused interest in every part of you – sexual, emotional, intellectual – and her eagerness to stimulate each of these facets of your being. A really good **Regular** can be depended upon, come hell or high water, and since your life always teeters on the edge of such possibilities, you can never have too many good **Regulars**. Just how many you can keep on your active file depends on how much stamina and cunning you are endowed with.

As a role model, you might consider Jack: if Oscars were awarded for efficient time-management by married WMs, there is no doubt that Jack, AKA Jack-The-Lad, would be a winner. The effortless ease with which he juggles his three categories of women, without causing any apparent stress or distress to any of them or to himself, is truly awesome.

Jack is a free-floating, free-thinking, freelance handyman. He advertises his services in a local newspaper thus:

JACK-OF-ALL-TRADES TAKES ON ALL YOUR HOUSEHOLD PROBLEMS: WONKY WIRING, PATCHY PLUMBING, BUSTED BOILERS, SAGGING SHELVING – YOU NAME IT, I CAN FIX IT! SHOULDER TO CRY ON OR TO CARRY COALS TO NEWCASTLE ALSO PROVIDED, IF REQUIRED.

This jaunty approach nets him a constant stream of enquiries from which, after an initial visit, Jack chooses those customers he wants to add to his list of **Regulars**. Now Jack is one of those rare creatures, a WM with a heart of gold (well, gold-plated anyway) and he chooses only the neediest cases, those he feels compassion for: the struggling young single mother, the lonely attractive widow, the harassed attractive housewife, the stressed attractive executive, etc. all of whom desperately need a handyman like him to deal with those tasks they can't handle. Jack is not greedy for money so he doesn't mind turning down some jobs that he knows will bore him – crotchety, critical pensioners or unattractive bossy matrons, for instance. Jack wisely does not tell his wife that he turns down jobs or that his clients are all attractive women: why worry her?

He has compassion for her too, what with three children, a part-time job *and* trying to do an Open University degree in the evenings! That's the way she is, likes to keep busy, doesn't believe work has to be fun, as he does. But he wouldn't change her for the world; a wife too busy to ask too many questions, that's fine with him! By trial and error, Jack has gradually worked out a perfect system which we can call: **ROTATING THE REGULARS**.

Because his customers have a habit of also becoming his playmates and because there is such a demand for his services, both professional and on the side, Jack allots specific days and intervals of time to specific clients in an unvarying rhythm which, unexpectedly and occasionally, he will break. For example: if he always visits Client A on Tuesday mornings for two hours every two weeks, he will suddenly change her to Thursday afternoons for one hour every week and re-assign Tuesday mornings every two weeks to Client B, his usual Thursday client. And so on, throughout his customer list, throughout the year. It may be hard to believe, but this system still allows Jack pockets of time which he can fill with the odd **Temp** or two, should he be so inclined.

By occasionally increasing or decreasing intervals of time between meetings with **Regulars**, Jack creates a kind of music, a hypnotic rhythm none of them can predict, keeping them on their toes. Although he himself knows exactly when and where he will appear next, he never makes precise verbal commitments, using the casual 'I'll call you' or 'I'll let you know' in preference to the completely naff 'Next Thursday at 5:30pm.'

Excuses

The powers of invention required to maintain credibility and some semblance of order in what is – let's face it – a chaotic life style, are not unlike those demanded of a great writer, painter or composer. A fertile creative imagination is essential to WM and must be assiduously exercised. Some WMs have become seriously stressed as a result of the huge cerebral effort imposed by the necessity of constantly inventing new and plausible excuses. To avoid becoming stressed, let your pleasures be guided by logic. And above all, *DON'T PANIC!* Panic is the problem. Break down your excuses into

the following categories:

1. **Excuses to The Primary**
2. **Excuses to Regulars**
3. **Excuses to Temps**
4. **Excuses to Anyone Else Connected to the Above**

It is Category 1 which challenges your inventiveness most of all. The minute a woman acquires the status of **Primary** in your life, she also acquires an extraordinary faculty which was not previously noticeable. It is the *Investigative Sense*, the ability to detect discrepancies in your excuses. This Sense becomes more acute with every day, every month, every year that a woman spends as your **Primary**. No wonder WMs change wives so often! However, you would be mistaken if you believe that the more marriages you have, the easier you will find the art of excuse-making: in fact, it is the latest wife who, with good reason, is the most suspicious of all and therefore the one you have to be the most creative for.

A strategy which rarely fails if you use it with subtlety is the *YOU'RE ABSOLUTELY RIGHT* ploy:

you make a point of agreeing with every one of the spouse's suspicions, even adding graphic detail (borrowed from the truth), weaving an elaborate tapestry of intrigue which can't possibly be true ...Or can it?

If you maintain a relaxed, good-humoured demeanour whilst describing this scenario, the effect on the woman is hypnotic and disorientating, causing her to lose confidence in her previous certainty of your guilt. She ends up feeling foolish, you forgive her foolishness, and all is well. Until the next time.

Excuses to **Regulars** do not usually require as much effort because their role in your life is fluid, ambiguous. And it is vital that you remind them of this as often as possible, especially if they ever become demanding. They must accept that they are not *entitled* to excuses from you and that it is only out of the goodness of your heart that you take the trouble, now and then, to give them explanations for your absences or cancellations. If you must come up with reasons there's no need to tax your brain unduly – you can simply improvise on the old standards: traffic, late trains, working late, baby-sitting, wife-sitting, etc. The good **Regular** will suspend her disbelief because you are *her* **WM**.

The bad **Regular** will have to be ditched.

Upgrading a good **Regular** to Spouse-status has often been tried but rarely works because, as you must remember: **SOONER OR LATER THE WORSHIP-FULNESS WEARS OFF**.

So you'd be wise to keep the class system in force, i.e. *EVERY WOMAN IN HER PLACE*.

Excuses to **Temps**, if made at all, should be quick and witty – like the encounters themselves.

Excuses to **Anyone Else** who becomes involved, wittingly or unwittingly, in your world-wide web of deceit could simply be sent out on the Internet: **WWW.TOWHOMITMAYCONCERN.WM.COM**

A vital lesson that every WM must learn is this: Every woman who falls for you – even if she pretends the contrary – believes that she, and she alone, will change you.

She thinks that – somehow, miraculously – you will become an **rm**, while still keeping your sexy WM charisma ... *BUT ONLY FOR HER!*

The fact that this is illogical and an

impossibility does not occur to her, or if it does, is seen as an obstacle which she can overcome.

DO NOT DISSUADE HER/THEM FROM THIS BELIEF!

The truth is less important than results and results are what you're after. A woman with a secret mission to change you becomes extremely resourceful in finding ways to please, excite and intrigue you. So don't take this away from her by stubbornly insisting that you will never change, no matter what she does. Keep this fact to yourself – let her find it out later rather than sooner.

10

PUNISHMENTS AND
TORTURES

Let's be clear: we're not talking corporal punishment here, whether of the battering kind or the S/M kind. If that's how you get your kicks, your problems have problems beyond the scope of this simple manual. WM should only use psychological punishments and mental tortures and then merely to stay in business – the business of **Worshipability**.

The longer a woman has been in your circle, the more likely she is to need regular punishment by way of maintenance. An unpunished worshipper is an untrustworthy worshipper. She may become restless, inattentive; but even if she is blameless, her commitment must be constantly tested. The punished need not always be told why they are being punished – in fact, punishment is far more effective if it is undefined, unexpected and undeserved. When you get that winsome, tearful, heartbroken *'BUT WHAT DID I DO WRONG?'* routine, you know that you are Master.

Like the art of inventing excuses, devising appropriate punishments requires no small expenditure of creative energy, so don't waste punishments on subjects you would rather not keep in your circle. Those that are judiciously punished tend to stick around for more of the same – call them masochists, call them schmasochists, as long as they worship you, it's alright!

Standard Punishments

1. The Big Sulk

Very effective for wives or any other women you spend considerable amounts of time with. The technique consists of silence – not just an ordinary silence, but a weighty, pregnant, meaningful silence whose meaning you are not prepared to

THE BIG SULK

divulge. You exude this silence whenever and wherever she can see you exuding it – sitting in your armchair, at table, in bed, in car / train / plane, on holiday etc.

She will repeatedly ask: 'What's the matter?' in increasingly anxious tones but you must never explain. Instead, you sigh – a deep, hopeless sigh.

Or you might snap: 'Let me have some space! Don't be so invasive!'

Or try: 'You wouldn't understand.'

And there's also: 'If you really cared about me, you wouldn't need to ask.'

She must be made to feel it's *her fault* that you're silent and sad and nothing she does can make up for her transgression. The longer you can keep up this punishment, the more powerful it is, the more unbearable to her. She will do anything to regain communication with you.

2. The Walk-Out

Useful when you're being cross-examined or when your wishes, decisions or opinions are being contradicted. A WM of Latin temperament might precede the Walk-Out with shouting and slamming of doors but this is unnecessary. A cool Frankly-My-Dear-I-Don't-Give-A-Damn exit packs a greater punch. How long you stay away is optional – could be a few hours, overnight, or a few days – whatever's needed to let the punishment sink in.

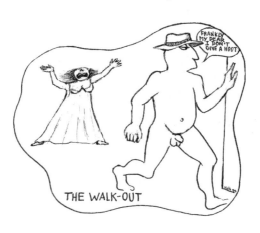

THE WALK-OUT

3. The Serious Threat

Similar to the **Walk-Out** but much more dramatic. All you need is a trigger: a wrong word from her is enough to start the process.

Allow the offending word to reverberate in the air for a while, building up the tension, then rise decisively (if you were sitting) and announce that you are leaving and not coming back – this is it, the end of the affair. For full effect, *YOU MUST ACTUALLY MEAN THIS* – even if you retract later. All women in love can sense when a man is just pretending to leave them for good. You must be a skilful enough actor to convince her this is really what you want to do. There is a very, very small risk that she could say: 'Well alright then, goodbye.' Much more likely, she will be on her knees, in tears, begging you to stay. Go, without saying where, and without communicating for a considerable length of time. Return without warning.

4. The Chastity Sting

This is an exquisitely painful punishment which works wonders for your libido. You begin by inviting the unsuspecting lover on a 'romantic' holiday, allowing her to build up expectations. Once arrived at the exotic, sensual location and in bed together, you give her a chaste kiss goodnight, turn your back and instantly fall asleep. She'll tell herself that you're exhausted, overworked, and all will be well as soon as you're rested. But the next morning, and for the rest of the holiday (which might last as long as two weeks), you repeat the performance, with variations. You do not explain why you are abstaining from sex with her, letting her imagination run riot with possible reasons: you're

THE CHASTITY STING

no longer turned on by her; you think she's too fat/thin/ugly/old; you're having an affair with someone else and only think about *HER*, etc. If she voices these fears, smile enigmatically, neither confirming or denying. If she becomes insistent or overtly lustful, accuse her of vulgar, un-feminine behaviour, saying that it's her demands that are turning you off. When you can see that the punishment has worked and she's been reduced to an inert, zombie-like creature, you can let up, relax and exercise your normal prerogatives.

TORTURES

Unlike **Punishments**, which should be carefully timed and reserved for special occasions, **TORTURES** are the **WM**'s stock-in-trade and can be used anytime, anywhere, as often as you like.

Here are just a few of the most popular tortures practised by WMs the world over. (Keep a record of any new ones you invent.)

1. SEX TORTURES

Knowing that you are widely and endlessly desired allows you to consolidate your power by a system of arousal and refusal, as illustrated under ADDICTABILITY. The expression 'making love' is totally inappropriate to describe WM's techniques of sexual Karate, designed to render the subject/conquest/victim helpless, confused and exhilarated.

A. TECHNO-SEX

You give her complicated, cool, strictly technical instructions relating to positions, movements, wearing-apparel, etc. This is torture to a woman who is desperately yearning for intimate, reciprocal, sentimental Soul-Bonding with you. It is *not* torture to those who are Techno-Sex freaks: don't get involved with them, they will only try to upstage you.

B. IRRELEVANCE

You choose a moment during sex when she's totally lost in passion, ready for the earth to move, the stars to fall and the chains of Love to tie you together forever and ever, to make a casual remark, such as: 'What time is that Panorama programme on?'

C. QUICK GET-AWAY

The instant after your orgasm you're up and into your clothes and out of there.

D. MIXED MESSAGE

You have a long, erotic, uncharacteristically intimate session with her and take your leave tenderly. Then you disappear for quite a while, a month or more, without calling her. When you return, it's only for a fast **Techno-Sex** bout, combined with b and c.

MIXED MESSAGE

E. IMPLIED RIVAL

You arrive at the rendezvous drunk, looking dissolute, debauched and dishevelled. You do not co-operate with her enquiries. You fall asleep while she is making love to you.

SNORE.. SNORE...

IMPLIED RIVAL

F. THE CLINTON

This works best if your attention is on something else at the time, such as speaking on the phone or writing.

You must not make a move, touch her or participate in any way. As soon as she has finished servicing you, she must leave without a word.

G. THE CRITIQUE

You explain, in detail, why you are not going to have sex with her this time: she has bought the wrong booze; prepared the wrong food; the lighting is wrong; the music is wrong; her hair and her clothes are wrong; she said the wrong

thing the minute you walked in and effectively killed your desire for her. You do not accept her apologies, reparations or recriminations.

THE COMPETITION TORTURE

2. COMPETITION TORTURE

She-Who-Is-With-You at the moment is given the not-inaccurate impression that she is only one of the contestants in a Miss World Competition of which you are the sole Judge and that, given the quality and quantity of the other competitors, she's got about as much chance of coming in first as she has of winning the Lottery jackpot. Since every woman, no matter how beautiful, clever or talented, is fundamentally insecure about the question: *AM I REALLY NUMBER ONE WITH HIM?* this manoeuvre, besides being fun for you, is also the most effective, slow-drip torture practised since time immemorial by WMs in all walks of life around the world. Whenever you are out with a woman – irrespective of whether she is your **Primary**, **Regular**, or **Temp** – and wherever you happen to be, at a party, in a restaurant, in a shop, or just walking down the street, never miss an opportunity to cast bold, invitational glances at every attractive woman and to engage her in bantering conversation, eliciting information about her. If your partner later protests, you can accuse her of being a straight-laced spoil-sport with no sense of humour and of wanting to tie you to her apron strings.

3. TELEPHONE TORTURES

No-one knows better than WM how to use the telephone as an instrument both of seduction and of torture. Here are some of the old favourites, never off the WM's best-sellers list:

A. Never say where you're calling from and make sure she can't trace it.

B. Phone her from another lover's bed and, while giving nothing away, make it obvious by the husky sound of your voice that you're up to no good.

C. Give her strict orders that she is *NEVER* to phone you. If she disobeys (as she is sure to do, sooner or later), make your response so brief, icy and cutting that she will feel sure she has lost you forever through her own foolish disobedience.

D. Never leave a message on her answering machine. She'll know the non-message was from you, reproaching her for not being there.

E. Do not phone her at all when you're sure she's longing for you to do so. Let her wait. And wait.

F. After a long period of NO-TEL, call her long distance and reverse the charges.

G. Phone her very late at night and pour out your troubles at length. She will urge you to come over at once so she can comfort you. Decline this offer, without saying where you are and hang up with a sigh. She will be unable to get back to sleep, worrying and fretting. You could keep this up for several hours – phoning back, talking some more, hanging up, waiting, calling again, etc.

H. After a long absence, phone and say you'll be over in an hour. During this hour, she will be excitedly preparing herself for your return. Two or three hours later, phone again to say that something urgent has come up and you won't be able to make it today. Apologise (but not too profusely), and hang up quickly before she has time to express her grievance. Whatever her style – dignified silence, explosive rage, quiet sobbing, sarcastic lecturing – you don't want and don't need to hear it. Besides, the torture is even sweeter if she's denied the opportunity to protest.

I. Use hypnotic suggestion, at a distance, but reverse the usual Positive Affirmations. Instead, try this: 'Every hour, every day, every week that *I DON'T PHONE YOU*, you sink deeper and deeper into self-doubt, insecurity, jealousy, frustration...' The beauty of this technique is that you, the Mesmerising Master, are in total remote-control of her mind and can instantly snap her back into joyous animation with just one 'Positive' phone call.

In about 1% of females addicted to WMs a prolonged period of NO-TEL torture has the effect of making them turn their attention to other matters or to other men. If this should happen to one of your women, don't lament the fact!

No woman is irreplaceable, especially if she's one of those who can't respond positively to punishment.

11

CHILDREN

Women and children do not, in reality, come first. You, WM, come first.

Children are competition. They are also embarrassing, financially disastrous, dependent, unreliable, dissident, nagging, clinging guilt machines.

You can never have too few. Or too many – for dubious support in your old age.

Make sure they have plenty of mothers to look after them.

GUILT

CONTRITION

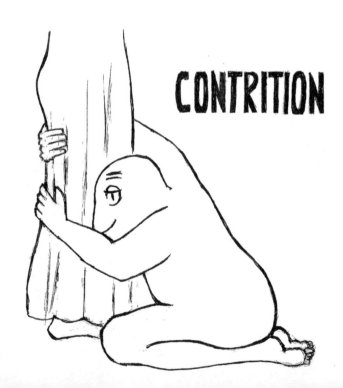

12

GUILT, CONTRITION
AND LOVEABILITY

Your life as WM gives you plenty of opportunities for guilt. As a WM, you must realise that opportunities is exactly what they are.

Guilt is frequently followed by remorse, the nagging *Why-Did-I-Do-That* feeling. This is not the same as **CONTRITION** (actually being sorry) which, when properly enacted, adds immeasurably to your **LOVEABILITY** rating.

Lines such as: *'It's all my fault...'* Or: *'I don't deserve you...'* Or: *'How can I change?'* may sound like worn-out clichés, but it's amazing how well-received they can be when spoken with sincere **CONTRITION**.

Do not confuse sincerity with decision-making. Your freedom to do mischief again is not really jeopardised by sincerity. You are sincere *at the time* of speaking, but who can predict what the future holds? For the time being, you are simply seizing an opportunity to add the **LOVEABILITY** factor to your credentials.

A caution: make sure your guilt occurs *after* the mischievous event and not before! If you allow guilt feelings to spoil your fun before you've even started, you are in serious danger of becoming one of the Enemy, i.e. rm. And then it's goodbye to the Carte Blanche of worshipability and CLANG! go the iron gates that make you the prisoner of your former worshippers. Remember that rm looks at you with resentment, envying your effortless ability to get away with murder while he suffers agonies of conscience over the least transgression. So do not give him the satisfaction of seeing you squirm in unseemly guilt *before* you get up to your misbehaviour.

If some people accuse you of sowing chaos wherever you go, be sincerely contrite about it. You can also ask them, humbly: is it not a charming chaos, bringing some excitement into humdrum lives? And is it not because they *need* a little of that sexy chaos in their predictable days and nights that they should forgive your occasional trespasses?

Building up your **LOVEABILITY** rating is no wimpish exercise in crowd-pleasing; no WM ever stoops that low. It is merely being practical and prudent and saving for that Rainy Day.

Because that Rainy Day does come, sooner or later, to every WM. There comes a point when guilt and opportunities for guilt accumulate and escalate and suddenly, it's all too much.

- You go into Little-Boy-Lost mode.
- You curl up in the foetal position and don't want to get out of bed in the morning.
- You miss your mother even if she was a bad mother and even if you never knew her.
- You ruminate about all the mistakes you made in your life.
- If you're a success you feel a failure and if you're a failure you feel an even worse failure.
- You feel helpless and frightened.

LOVEABILITY

Helplessly you wander, lonely as a cloud, from woman to woman in your circle. And if you were sexy when radiating confidence, your Little-Boy-Lost mode arouses raging maternal instincts in every female from six to well-past senior citizenship.

The more lost you are, the higher climbs your **LOVEABILITY** rating. You look unshaven, unwashed, grey, ill, wonderful. The women's hearts turn over and bleed for you.

You ask them for solace and advice: 'Why do I mess everything up?' 'What's wrong with me?' 'What should I do?'

The women give you heartfelt counselling, hot coffee, hot baths, chicken soup, haircuts, tender sex, whatever you need. You thank them, sincerely, tell them they are wise, smile sadly with your Little-Boy-Lost eyes and wander off, still lonely as a cloud.

Until the Rainy Days pass, as they do. And Rosie days are here again.

13

LOOSE WOMEN

Loose Women are those who are running around un-caught, un-affected by and unaware of your power.

This cannot be allowed.

They should have the chance to experience you at least once in their lives.

Loose Women are everywhere: they are the ones who do not give you the eye, do not respond to your glance, do not laugh at your jokes, do not strike up a conversation with you. The women who do all those things are already in the bag, hooked, lined up and ready to be sunk. But the **Loosies** are equivalent to virgins in the hierarchy of desirability.

Other women will always be waiting for you

but a **Loosie** might get away before you've even tried to catch her. So you have to adapt your tactics to the prey.

Let us call one of these **Loosies** 'Rosie'.

When you first notice her, Rosie is with a friend of hers. You begin by ignoring Rosie. You pay close attention to the friend, carefully avoiding eye-contact with Rosie and if you speak to her at all it is with polite indifference. You cultivate the friend and contrive to discover where Rosie works or hangs out. You then manufacture occasions to be in the same place and you 'accidentally' run into Rosie but continue to treat her in a cool, off-hand manner. This game requires patience as it can be quite slow but it is very rewarding if you persist.

Eventually, Rosie is piqued by your indifference and her curiosity is aroused: Who is this man: *WHY* does he ignore me? What do all these women see in him? I will find out.

And presto! She has walked into the trap. From there on you can just play it by ear. Once trapped, a **Loosie** tames very quickly and, indeed, becomes very difficult to shake off. You may be an acquired taste to her, but once acquired, it's one she cannot do without. She clings, like cling-film. And if you're wrapped in cling-film...

By all means catch a **Loosie** for the thrill of the hunt, but once you have caught her, always let her go.

14

THE ENEMY: MALE

WM's enemies are of two kinds:
MALE and **FEMALE**.

Your **MALE ENEMIES** are:

1. REFORMED WM

One who got himself into a lot of legal, financial or sexual trouble and was forced to 'seek help' of a psychological, spiritual or Alternative kind which caused him to become insufferably pompous, pedantic and patronising. He now runs a Centre called *WAM* (Worshipped Anonymous Men) where others like him regularly meet and confess their WM sins, applauding and shouting *'WAM!'* after every shameful revelation. He is constantly offering to 'help you', he understands you, he used to be just like you, but now the scales have dropped from his eyes...etc. etc. Tell him in no uncertain terms that the only scales you want to drop are those that show your weight.

2. WANNABE WM

Desperately aspires to *be* you but hasn't a ghost of a chance, just hasn't got what it takes. Follows you around like a puppy, imitates (ineptly) your behaviour and swears eternal loyalty to you. DO NOT TRUST HIM! He's the sort who will insinuate himself into your life, spy on you, then one fine day when you've kicked him out, write a slanderous book about you pretending he was your closest associate, the only one who knows the *truth* about you.

3. OTHER WMs

In the sex-war, there's only room for one WM in a woman's life and chances are she's too enthralled by you to fall simultaneously under the spell of another WM.

OTHER WMs

In the unlikely event of this happening, urge the woman to go to your rival. In fact, do your best to arrange this. Faced with this proof that you don't mind handing her over to another WM (or even sharing her) she will do her utmost to demonstrate that you are her One and Only. Ascertain that this is really so and that you have the only key to her heart and soul. Then send her off as a gift to your rival: you'll be one-up on him since he'll only have her body while you retain possession of all the rest.

In the success and fame stakes, other WMs could be a threat. However, keep the Ace of Sex card up your sleeve and use it whenever mere ruthless competitiveness is not enough – there will always be a woman you have that the other WM wants.

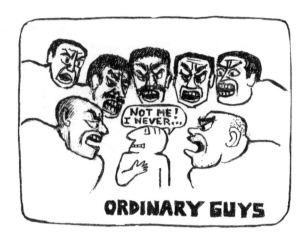

ORDINARY GUYS

4. ORDINARY GUYS (OGS)

Men who are neither WMs or rms are **OGS**. They are not, generally speaking, a danger to you unless they operate in groups, gangs, clans or committees. For instance, if they are the fathers, brothers or husbands of foreign girls you have indiscreetly dallied with. Or the mates of some lout in a pub whose girlfriend made eyes at you. Or the straight-laced family-values citizens you have somehow outraged by your unconventional lifestyle. In all such cases, the **OGS'** revenge is collective and highly emotional, not to say prejudiced. Your best defence is evasion – either literally running away from the scene, and/or dealing with it from a distance, via the best lawyers you can get.

5. GAY MEN

Not usually your enemies unless they fall in love with you, in which case they are likely to behave exactly like the women who fall in love with you (see **FEMALE ENEMIES**).

6. THE RM

Finally, the most innocent-looking but also the most dangerous enemy you have is RELIABLE MAN. Deep inside, he is consumed with envy yet he makes a point of having no time for you. He pretends to find you irrelevant, insensitive, infantile and ...wait for it: *BORING!* He should be so boring! Doesn't he notice all those gorgeous, clever women flocking around you? He claims to be baffled by your success with women. Baffled is not a problem – what *is* a problem is when he tries to influence your women with his priggish attitude, his 'New Manliness', his pretended equality with them. *EQUALITY?* In his dreams! All the women know they are far *superior* to him although, out of kindness, they hide it from him. They flock to you to feel *unequal, inferior, worshipping!* Never will **rm** be able to accept or understand this fact, not in a million years of reliability, equality and paternity. However, much as you can enjoy mocking him, you must never underestimate the threat that **rm** poses to your status. Your privileged position as WM can never be 100% secure so long as **rm** exists and so long as

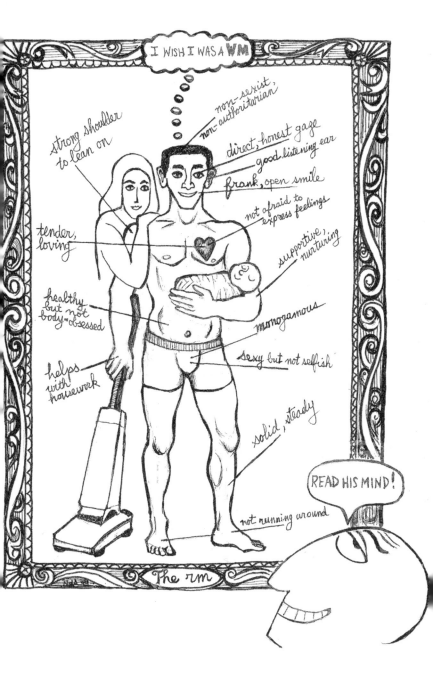

this equation remains unsolved:

<u>WOMEN WANT A WORSHIIPABLE MAN</u>
WOMEN WANT A RELIABLE MAN

In the balance of power, if you're the top, **rm** is zero. That's fine but it doesn't stay that way. If he's the top, you're powerless. That is unacceptable. Your best bet is to ensure that things stay at the **Impossibility Level** where they've always been – i.e. the state of confusion in women's minds as to what they want. Keep a cold war going and find subtle ways to undermine **rm**'s credibility. And, of course, try temptation: exactly how reliable is he? Would he turn down a chance, all expenses paid, to sample your lifestyle for a night or a week? If he falls once he can fall again and pretty soon he could be asking for lessons in **Addictability**! But if he can't be bribed or corrupted, there's always **THE RECAPTURE STING**, beautifully illustrated by the following case:

Belinda, married to WM Bruno, cannot cope with his WM ways and, after much crying and gnashing, decides to leave him. Bruno is none too pleased, he hadn't finished with her yet, but it's not his style to hang on so he lets her go. A divorce takes place and time goes by. Belinda, recovered from her trauma, meets a nice **rm** and marries him. Bruno, forgiven and forgiving, attends the wedding and blesses the new couple. More time goes by. One day, apparently on an impulse, Bruno phones Belinda for a friendly chat; he suggests that they meet for a drink as he wants to ask her help on a business idea. She agrees. Coincidentally, her husband happens to be away that day (Bruno knows this; Belinda doesn't know he knows). They meet at a bar and all the while they are discussing mundane matters, Bruno fixes her gaze with that Old Black Magic *you-and-I-alone-together* look. Belinda squirms, tries to avoid the gaze, but with each drink it becomes more difficult until finally, she is looking back at him in exactly the same way. Taking command, Bruno leads her outside, into his car, and back to his place (having ensured beforehand that he will not be disturbed). With lots of For-Old-Time's-Sake jesting and jousting, Bruno removes Belinda's

THE RECAPTURE STING

clothes and the last of her scruples and before you can say 'You've been framed!' they're at it like there's no tomorrow. As soon as she has said the necessary words: *'YOU'RE THE ONLY ONE I EVER REALLY LOVED'*, it's over.

Bruno cheerfully drives the flushed and guilty adulteress back to her legitimate conjugal home, says goodbye with a quick, cool peck on the cheek and no intention of ever seeing her again (unless, of course, *she* initiates it).

Bloodless battle won. Ex-runaway wife recaptured without a struggle and without the need to re-marry. Superiority over **rm** proved beyond a doubt. Mission accomplished.

15

THE ENEMY: FEMALE

To make sure that you have absorbed the previous lessons, herewith a re-cap of the most dangerous women:

1. THE JEALOUS
Every woman you're seeing/dating/screwing/ having an affair/a fling/a relationship with is jealous of every other woman in your past, present and future. This is unavoidable. However, it is the degree, the intensity of her jealousy which determines whether a particular woman becomes *THE ENEMY* or stays in the ranks of common-or-garden female, all buzz and no bite. For the mosquito to turn into a deadly snake, certain character-traits must have existed in the woman

before you ever met her. How can you tell if she has these traits? That's the problem: you can't! No early-warning system has yet been devised to protect the unsuspecting WM from potentially lethal jealous women. Might you be the one to discover such a system?

2. THE SCORNED

Those you used (well, that's how *they* put it; you could say: gave happiness to) for a while and then discarded. Also those whose advances you spurned, either because you didn't fancy them or because you guessed they were too dangerous. Hell definitely hath no fury like this lot and hell on earth is precisely what you can expect from them.

3. THE BETRAYED

Similar to the above but even worse. They are the ones you married, or otherwise seriously tangled with in business or pleasure, who naively trusted in your integrity. Until the day that they stumbled upon evidence of your secrets, your betrayal. Truly naive women are rare nowadays but if it has been your fortune/misfortune to shack up or do business with one, you are in for a big surprise. No sooner does she find out that you have double-crossed her than she becomes, overnight, a raging Joan of Arc. Her naivety and your betrayal fuse and ignite in her a passionate resolve, a mission to destroy you and avenge her stolen innocence. She will go to any lengths – including burning herself and/or you and your paramour at the stake (or steak-house, where she found you out). Or, less melodramatically but equally passionately, she will pursue you through the law-courts until she has extracted every last drop of blood, money or reputation from you.

4. THE ANGRY YOUNG WOMAN

One who vociferously disapproves of you, on principle. She could be someone you know well – your daughter, for instance – or a friend/relative of a woman you have 'wronged'; or she might even be a complete stranger. Everything about you seems to provoke her random rage, expressed in long-winded invective frequently backed up by feminist quotes. She may or may not be a lesbian.

If she has boyfriends, they tend to be of the unisex non-specific gender sort. She would vigorously reject any overtures from you but might, if drunk, pick you up for a quickie, immediately after which every detail of your performance and your anatomy will be raucously reported to her friends. Far from being a WM to her, you are a figure of fun and a target for her multitudinous frustrations. What she needs is a good spanking but DO NOT attempt to administer one!

5. THE CYNICAL OLDER WOMAN (COW)

She has lost her looks and her illusions, moved out of town, perhaps acquired a young **rm** lover or retired in sulky isolation. In her youth, she may have married one or more WMs. She may or may not know you personally but she knows all about *your type* and has made a career out of slashing you to bits with her razor-sharp gossip. Or she might be an eccentric old recluse, ranting about you to her cats when taking a break from sending you anonymous poison-pen letters. Or – and this is a distinct possibility – she is your mother.

6. THE FEMINIST

Whatever title she chooses to go by, she is a member of the most dangerous cult of our time. Depending on her age and geographical location, she will have had her 'consciousness' (and possibly other parts of her anatomy) raised. What this means in plain English is that she's after your balls.

Brain-washed by a small coterie of publicity-hungry, aggressively cerebral persons of the female gender (either jaded by over-indulgence or bitter because they could never indulge) and by a diet of women's magazine-speak in which **'orgasm'** and **'organic'** guarantee high circulation, this dangerously deluded creature goes round spreading the myth that you are dead, obsolete, finished, kaput, refusing to accept the incontrovertible evidence that you are not only very much alive but also energetically pursued by considerable numbers of her sisters. When she can spare the time from her frenetic pursuit of self-realisation and wants a change from her preferred menu (auto-eroticism, followed by same-sex sex, followed by a dose of chastity), she turns to **rm** as the acceptable male, for purposes of sex, sperm, social standing and/or security.

But not to worry too much. You can take comfort in this age-old certainty:

AS LONG AS WOMEN ARE WOMEN AND MEN ARE MEN

A SMALL NUMBER OF MEN WILL BE WORSHIPPED

AND A LARGE NUMBER OF WOMEN WILL BE WORSHIPPERS(*)

(*) Footnote: What will happen if the Feminists prevail doesn't bear thinking about.

AFTERWORD

So, **WM**, is it all going to end in tears?
No way, no fears!
If there's at least one women left on this planet
Some Jane or Janet
Who needs to worship a man
You'll be fine.

But you'll have to stand in line.